HOW TO DRAW
EVERYTHING
WHATABURGER

for kids

ALLI KOCH

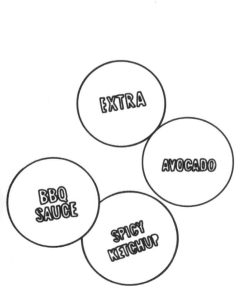

Blue Star Press.

Copyright © 2024 Whataburger
Published by Blue Star Press
PO Box 8835, Bend, OR 97708
contact@bluestarpress.com
www.bluestarpress.com

Written and illustrated by Alli Koch

ISBN: 9781963183047

Printed in Colombia

10 9 8 7 6 5 4 3 2 1

this book

BELONGS TO

_____

LET'S DRAW!

The nice thing about being an artist is that you make the rules. Everyone has their own style, which is why your drawings will look different from someone else's. In this book, each project is broken down into steps. My goal is to help you see the simple parts of what may seem like a hard thing to draw.

We will start with the most basic outline or guide and work our way up. You will start to see a pattern with each project we draw; starting with simple guidelines, then breaking down "C" and "S" shape lines, and lastly erasing the unneeded lines for the finished look. Don't forget to draw your lines lightly first so it is easier to erase them. My favorite thing to say when drawing is:

If it was perfect, it would not look handmade!

I cannot wait for you to get started. Happy drawing!

TOOLS

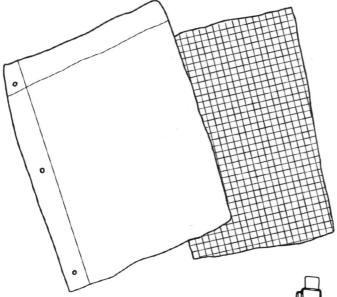

The cool thing about art is that you can use any tool you want! Yep, that's right! You are the artist, so feel free to be creative. For this book, let's keep it simple. It's easy to learn using either blank sheets of paper or grid paper.

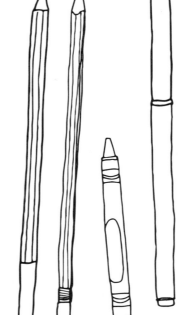

When you are learning to draw, you really only need a pencil and a good eraser. To follow the step-by-step instructions: draw everything lightly, then go over your lines with whatever tool you would like to use. You could use different pens, markers, colored pencils, or even crayons to add details to your drawings.

CIRCLES CAN BE TRICKY. TRY USING A PENNY OR A CIRCLE STENCIL TO HELP!

BREAK IT DOWN

Anyone can draw! If you can write your ABCs (which I am pretty sure you can do!), then you can draw everything in this book. Each drawing can be broken down into a bunch of "C" and "S" shaped lines. Almost everything that is round is two simple "C" lines put together. An "S" line is used when something has a dip or curvy line.

Most of the projects in this book are broken down into six or eight steps. What you will draw in each step will be a black line; what you have already done will be in gray lines. There are more than 40 fun Whataburger-inspired projects for you to learn how to draw. The chapter dividers in this book are also bonus coloring pages that you can color!

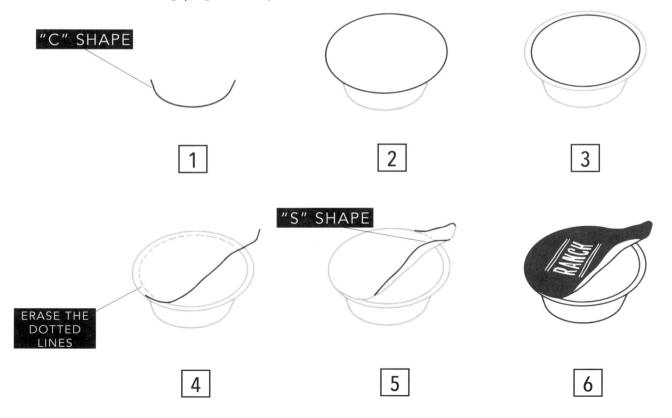

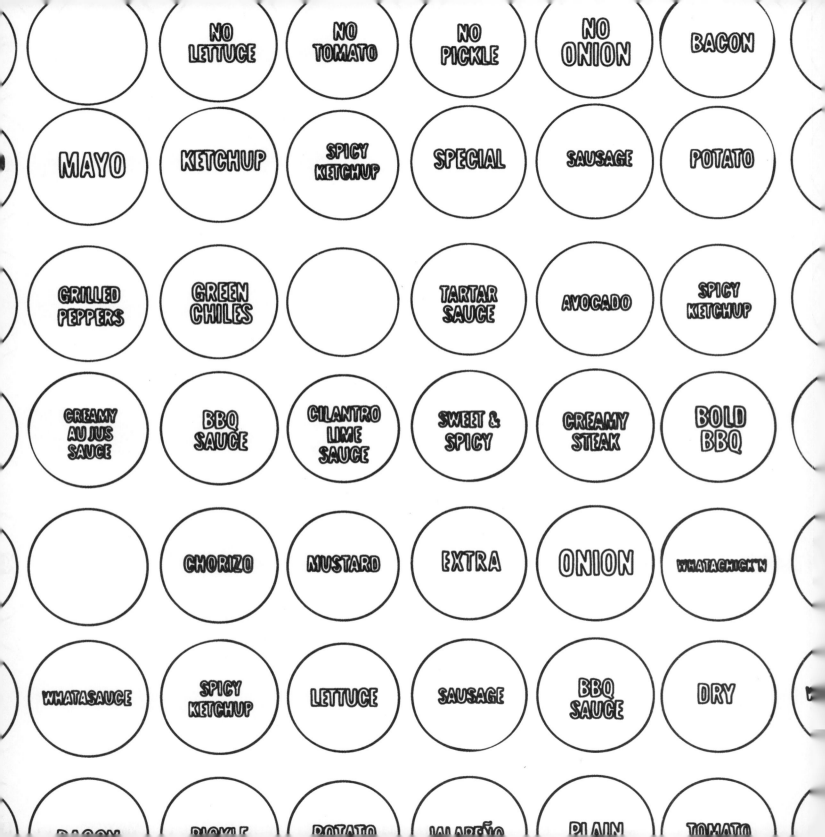

NO LETTUCE

NO TOMATO

NO PICKLE

NO ONION

BACON

JA

BBQ SAUCE

KETCHUP

SPECIAL

POTATO

A

SAUSAGE

GREEN CHILES

GRILLED PEPPERS

TARTAR SAUCE

AVOCADO

SPICY KETCHUP

ON THE MENU

PICKLE

MUSTARD

EXTRA

ONION

K

SPICY KETCHUP

LETTUCE

SAUSAGE

BACON

WHATABURGER

The world's largest burger fed 8,000 people!

1

2

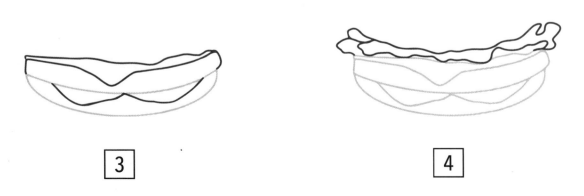

3

4

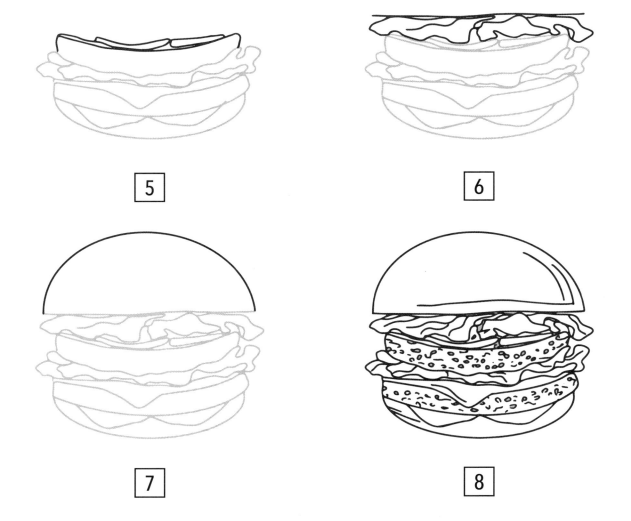

5

6

7

8

FRENCH FRIES

Russet potatoes make the best french fries due to their starch content.

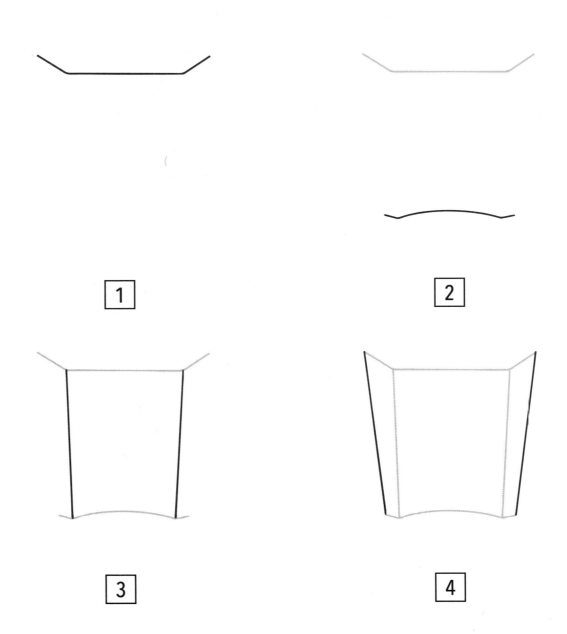

5

6

7

8

TOMATOES

Tomatoes come in other colors than just red. Some are also grown to be yellow, pink, purple, black, and even white!

1

2

3

4

5

6

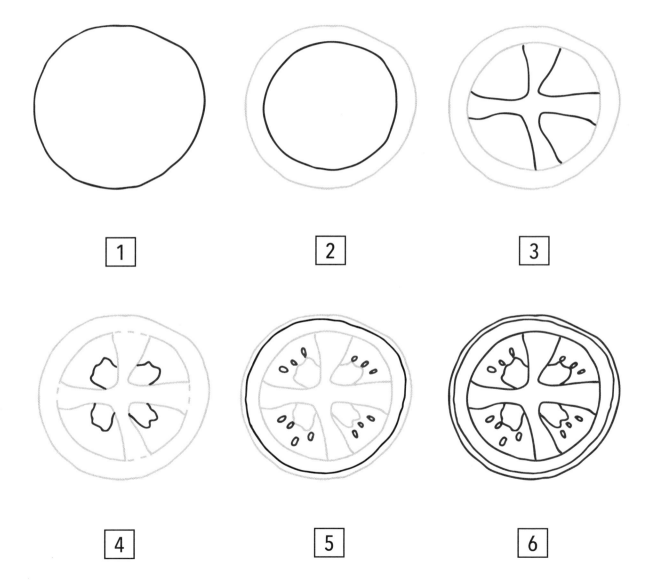

1   2   3

4   5   6

15

ONION RINGS

The first-ever recipe for onion rings appeared in an ad in a *New York Times* magazine that was published in 1933.

1

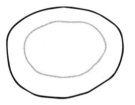

2

3

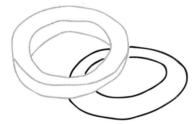

4

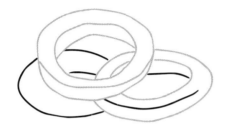

5

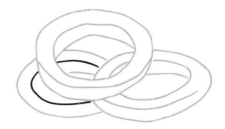

6

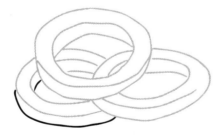

7

8

AVOCADOS

Avocados are technically a fruit and are thought to have originated in south-central Mexico.

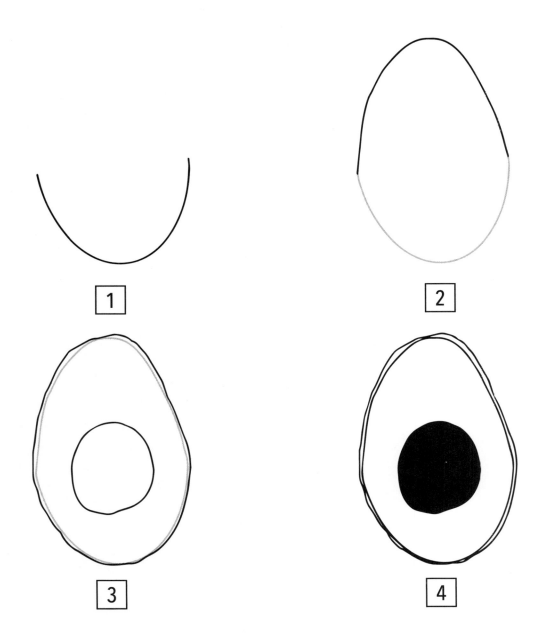

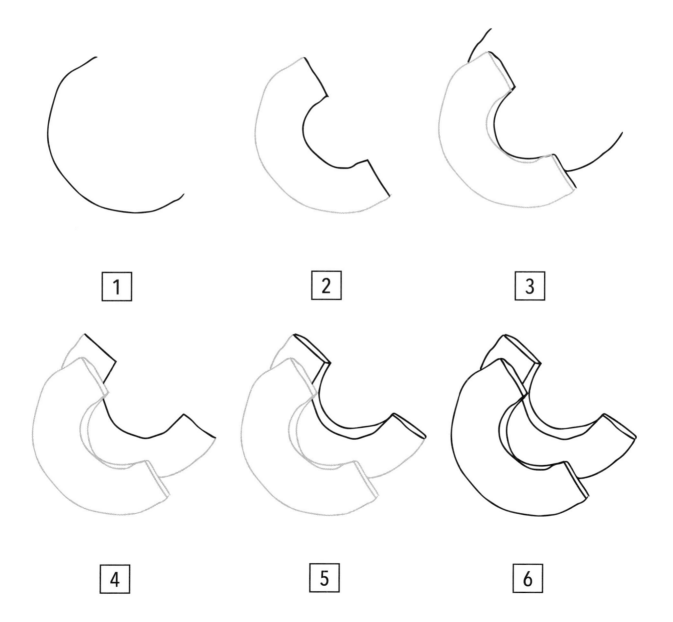

1

2

3

4

5

6

PICKLES

The term "pickle" comes from the Dutch word "pekel," which means salt or brine.

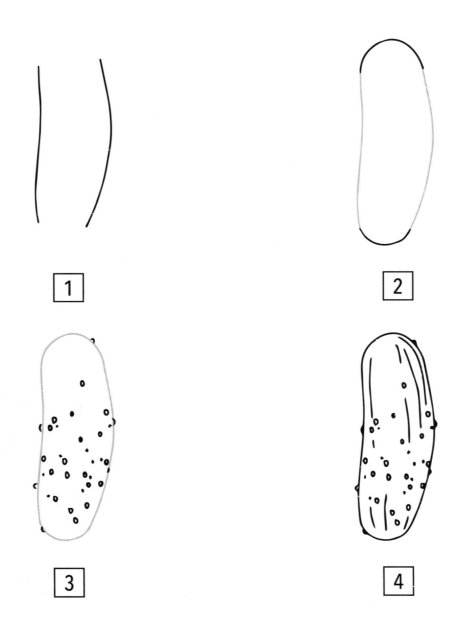

1

2

3

4

5

6

21

JALAPEÑOS

Whole jalapeño peppers are technically considered berries because they have many tiny seeds inside.

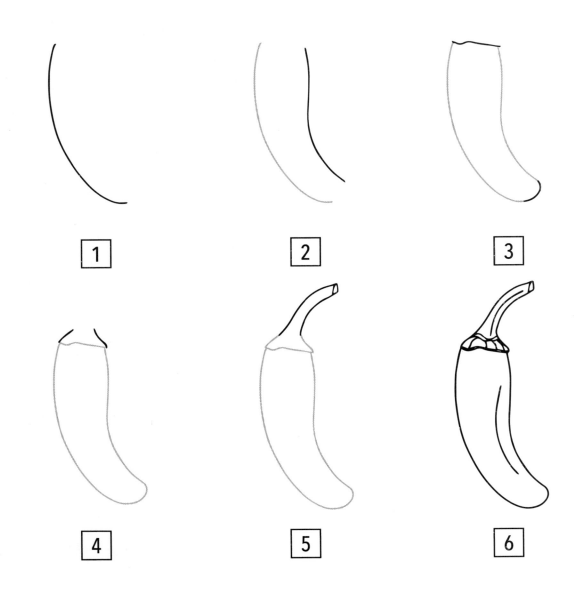

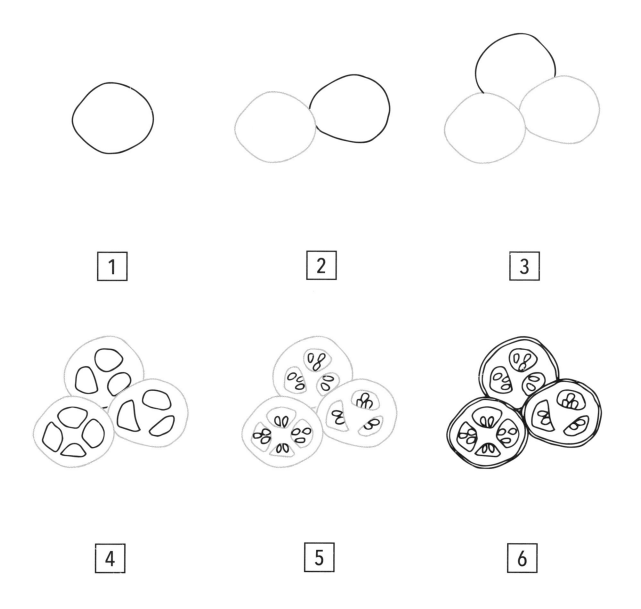

1

2

3

4

5

6

23

MUSTARD BOTTLE

Mustard is the leading spice worldwide, but the United States consumes more of it than any other country.

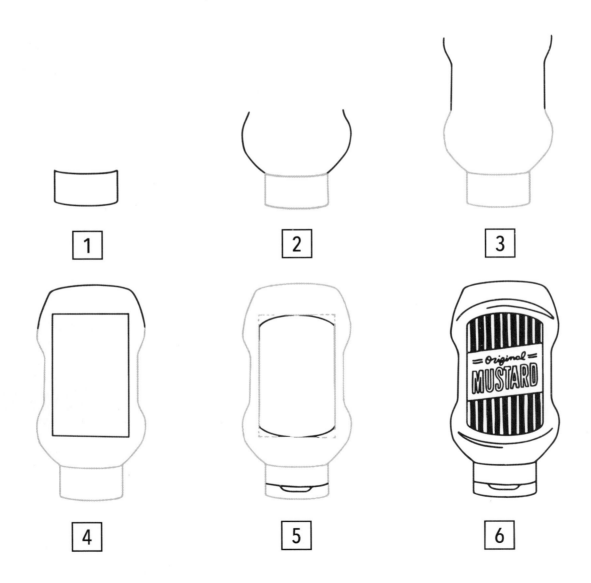

KETCHUP

Ketchup was originally inspired by a Chinese condiment, and the early recipes didn't even contain tomatoes.

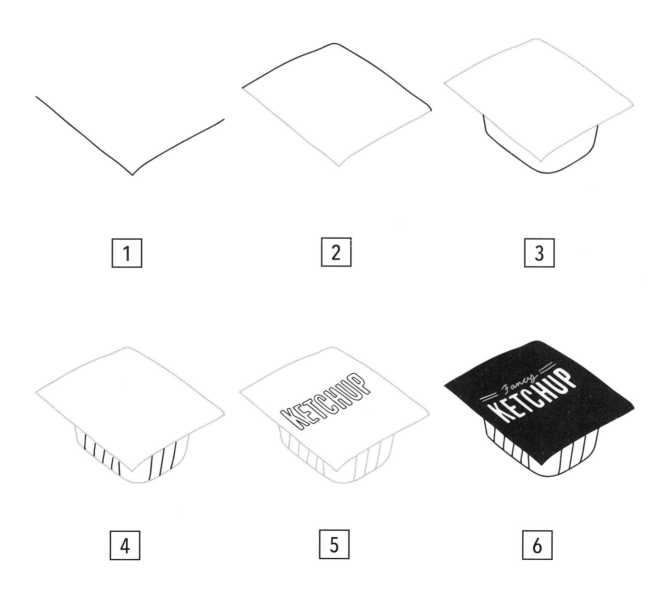

PATTY MELT

Whataburger's Patty Melt—a toasted sandwich with two beef patties, grilled onions, and cheese—is a fan favorite.

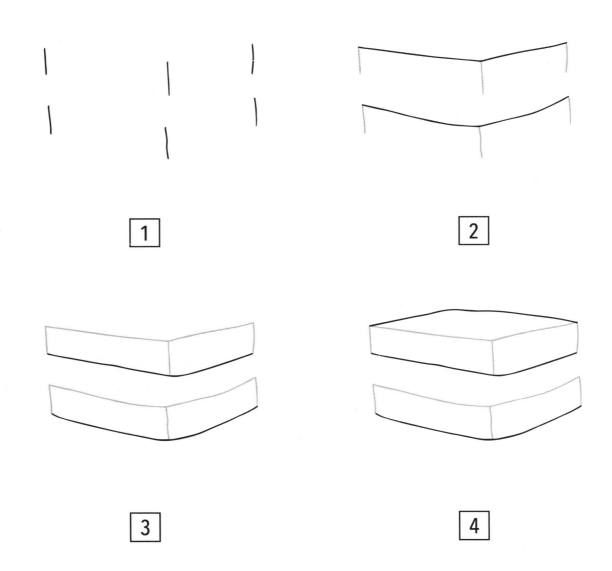

1

2

3

4

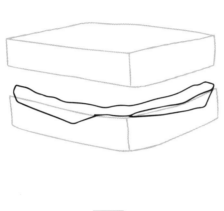

5

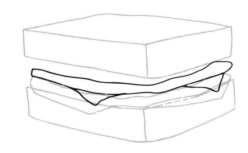

6

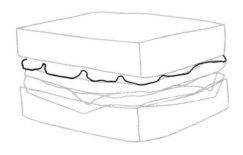

7

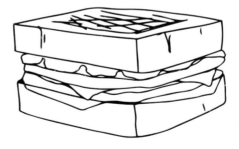

8

MILKSHAKE

The blender was invented in 1922 specifically for making milkshakes.

1

2

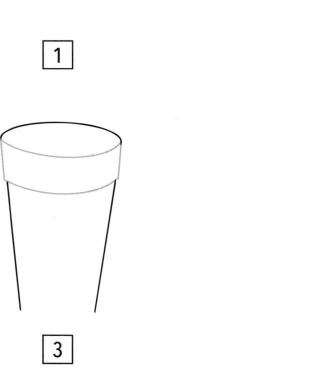

3

4

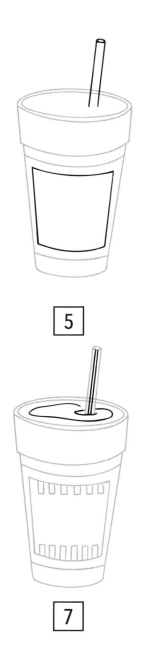

5

6

7

8

HONEY BUTTER CHICKEN BISCUIT

For every Wednesday game, the minor league baseball team in Whataburger's hometown changes its name from the Corpus Christi Hooks to the Corpus Christi Honey Butter Chicken Biscuits.

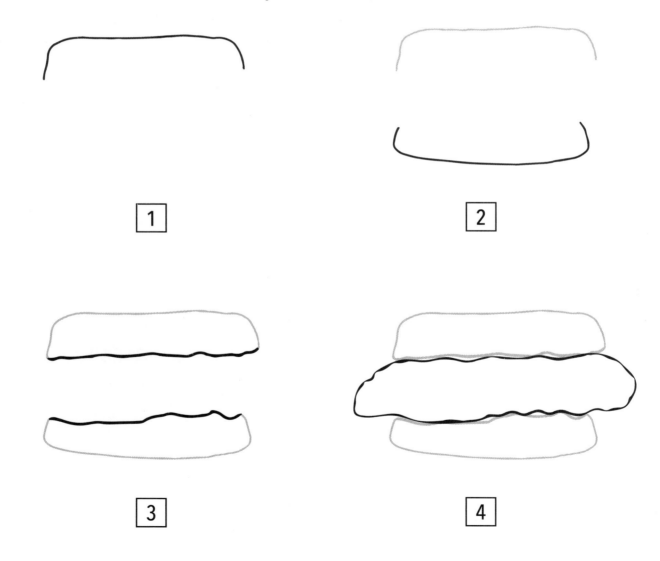

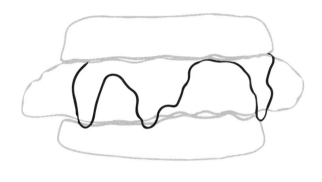

5

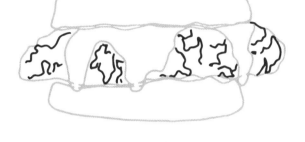

6

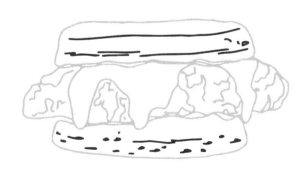

7

8

PANCAKES

The world's largest pancake was cooked in Rochdale, England, in 1994, measuring over 49 feet wide. It also weighed 3 tons (the same weight of an African elephant!).

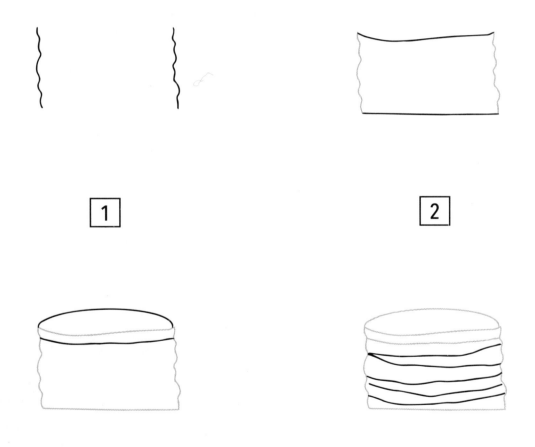

1

2

3

4

5

6

7

8

TAQUITO

The word "taquito" translates to "little taco" in Spanish.

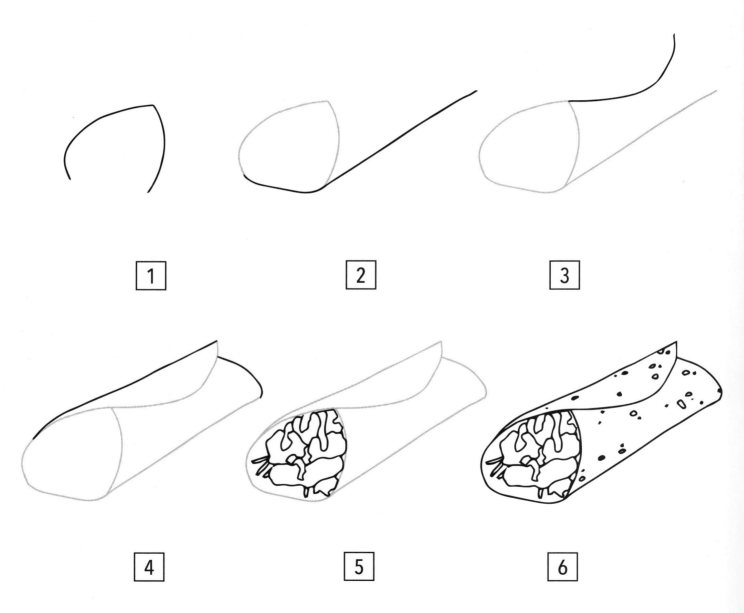

1

2

3

4

5

6

CINNAMON ROLL

Europeans brought the recipe for cinnamon rolls to Philadelphia when they immigrated to America.

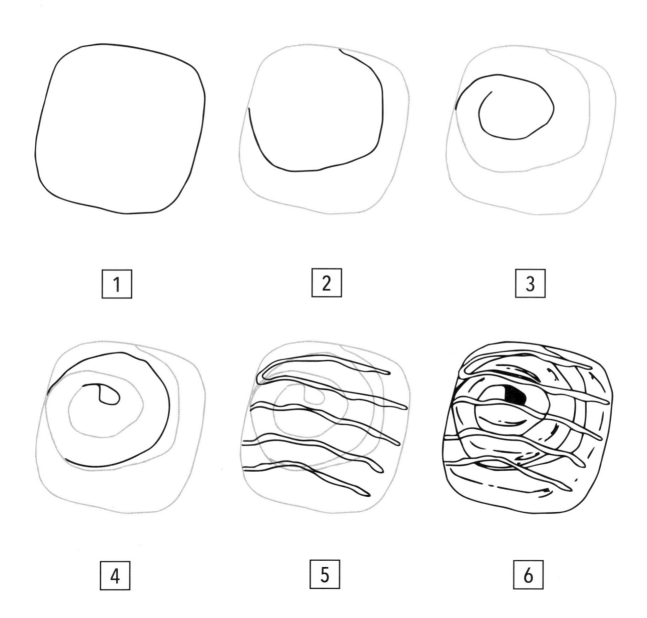

1

2

3

4

5

6

APPLE PIE

The largest apple pie ever made weighed over 18,000 pounds!

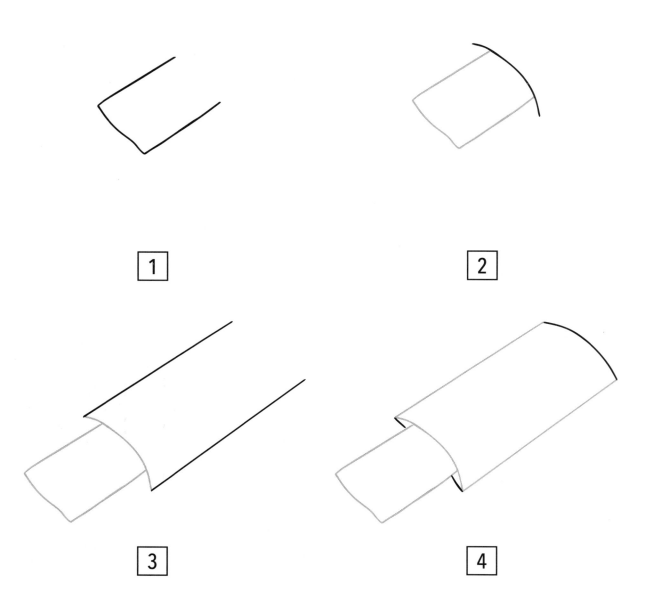

1

2

3

4

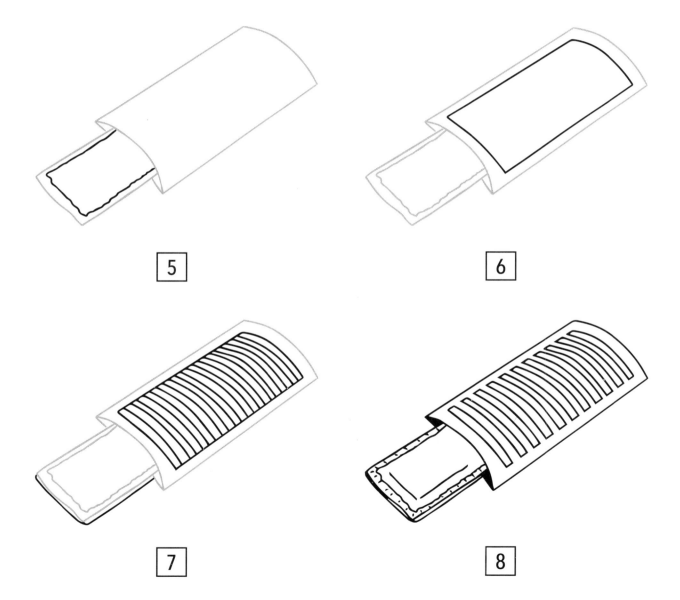

5

6

7

8

WHATABURGER LOGO

Following a design contest in 1973, Whataburger chose Corpus Christi artist Will Clay's "Flying W" as its logo.

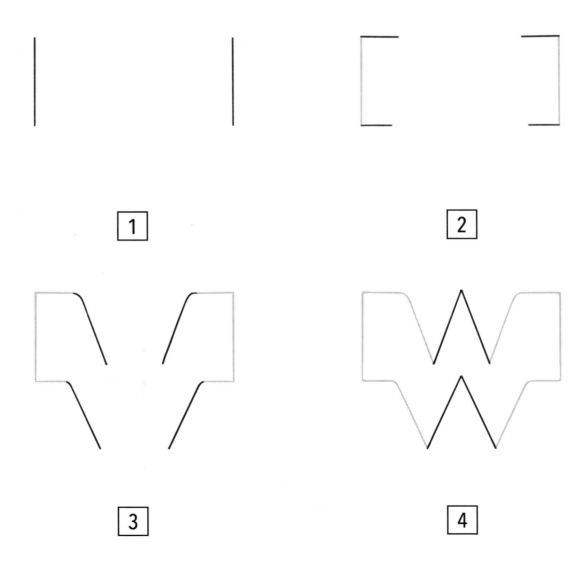

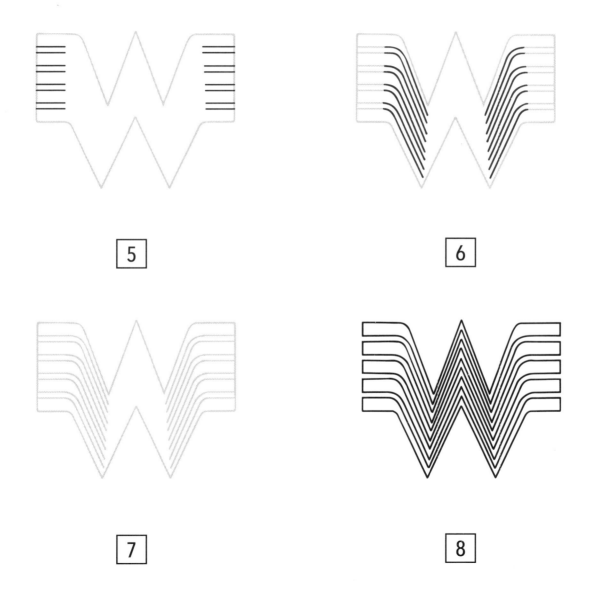

5

6

7

8

A-FRAME RESTAURANT

The distinct A-frame design of Whataburger's restaurants was inspired by founder Harmon Dobson's love of flying.

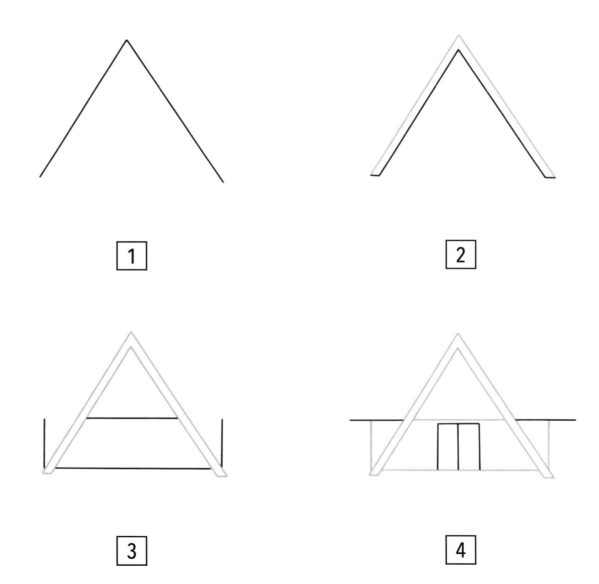

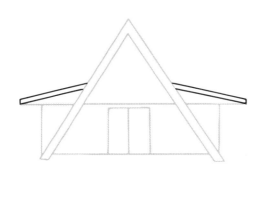

5

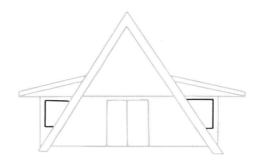

6

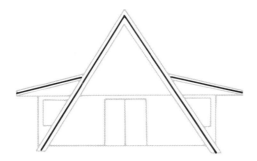

7

8

FOOD TRUCK

Whataburger's first restaurant was actually a portable stand, similar to a modern-day food truck.

1

2

3

4

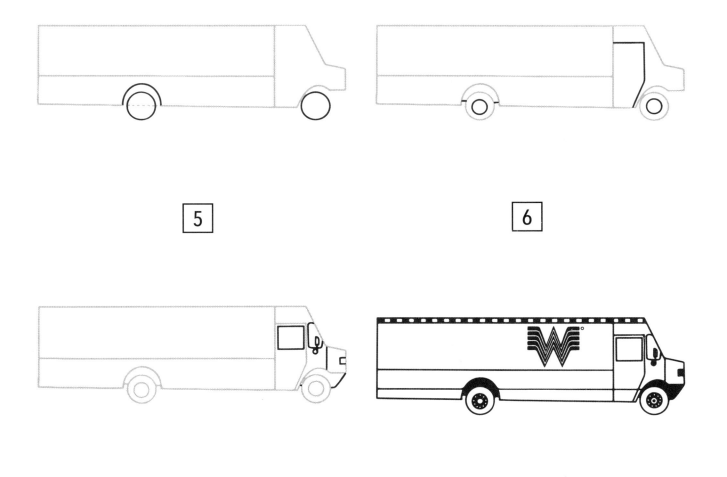

5

6

7

8

TABLE TENT

Whataburger's popular table tents are given to customers as they wait for their food to be delivered in the restaurant.

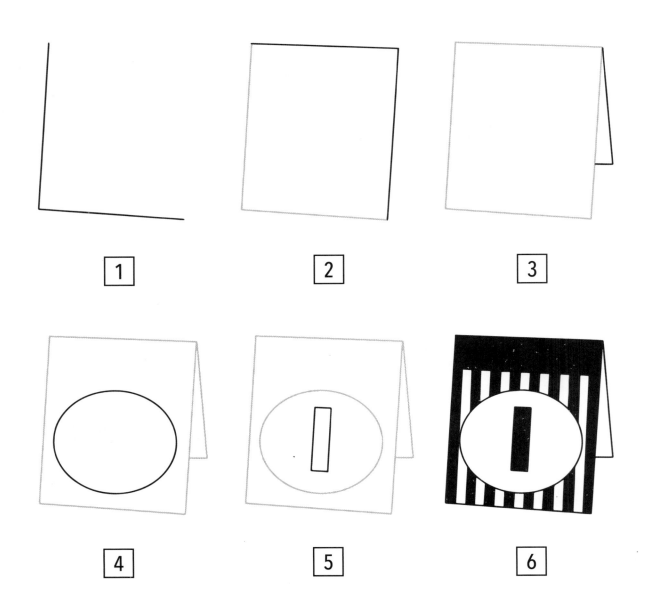

TO-GO BAG

While it got its start in Texas, today Whataburger is enjoyed by food lovers nationwide. And in 2025, Whataburger will celebrate its 75th anniversary!

1

2

3

4

5

6

TO-GO CUP

When you're done with your drink, you can repurpose your Whataburger cup by decorating it and cutting a small slot in the lid to create a unique piggy bank for saving coins and bills.

1

2

3

4

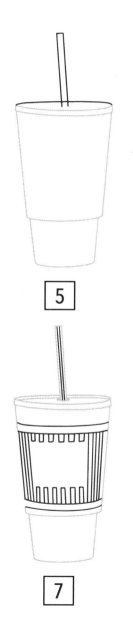

5

6

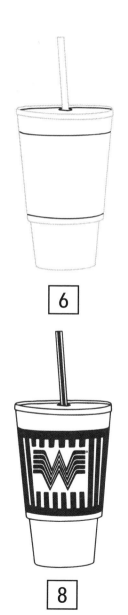

7

8

FOOD BOX

Did you know? You can also repurpose your food box and turn it into a simple musical instrument, like a shaker or drum, by filling it with small objects like beads or dried beans.

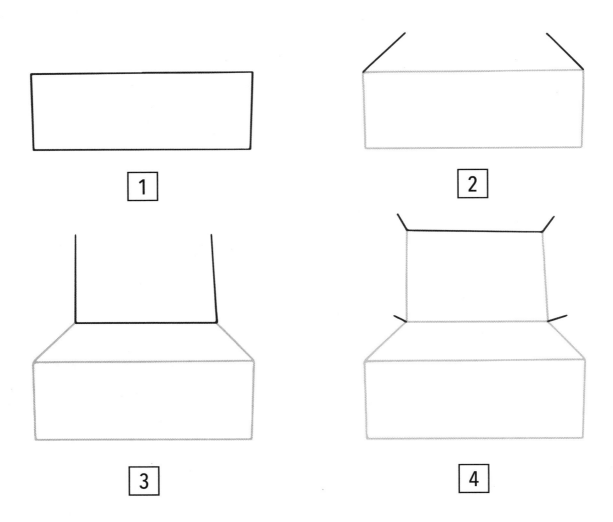

1

2

3

4

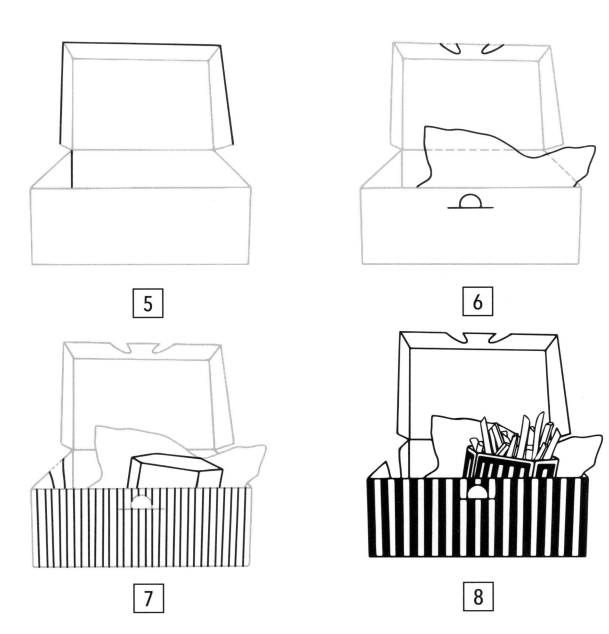

5

6

7

8

THE FANS

DOG

A dog's sense of smell can be up to 100,000 times more acute than a human's.

| 1 | 2 | 3 |

| 4 | 5 | 6 |

7

8

9

10

11

12

LONGHORN

One of the heaviest longhorns ever weighed a total of 2,045 pounds!

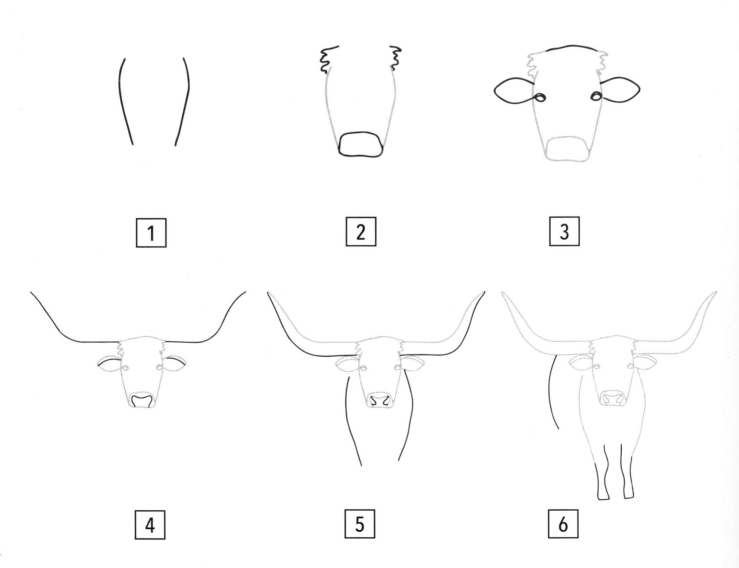

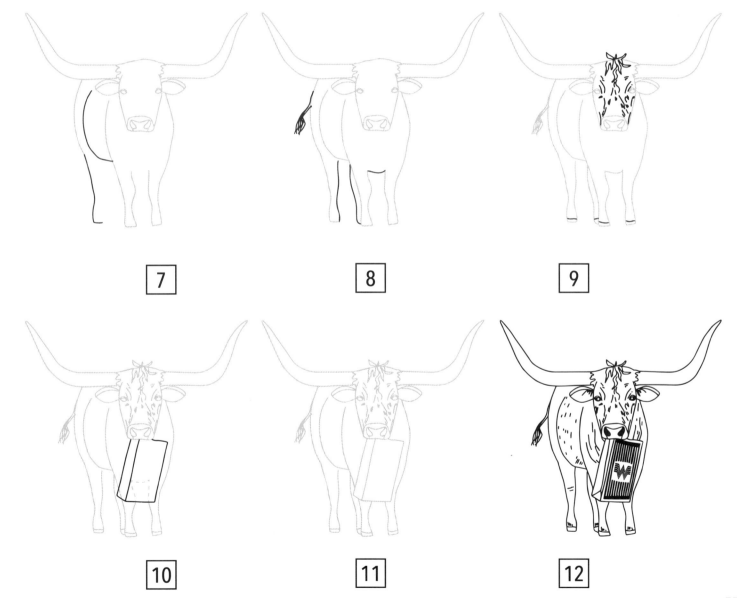

7

8

9

10

11

12

RATTLESNAKE

Rattlesnakes hear through vibrations rather than airborne sounds. Their inner ears are directly connected to their jaws.

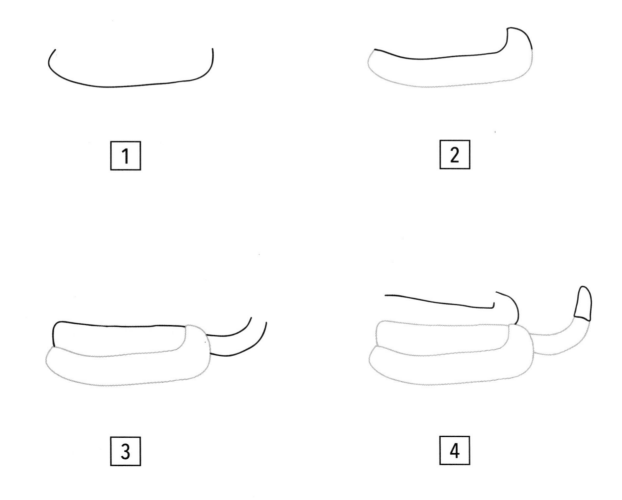

1

2

3

4

5

6

7

8

TEXAS

Whataburger's headquarters is located in San Antonio, Texas, and the company has a strong presence across the state.

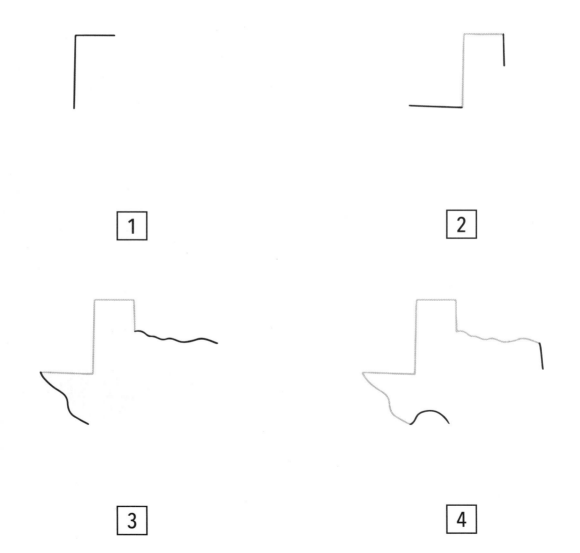

1

2

3

4

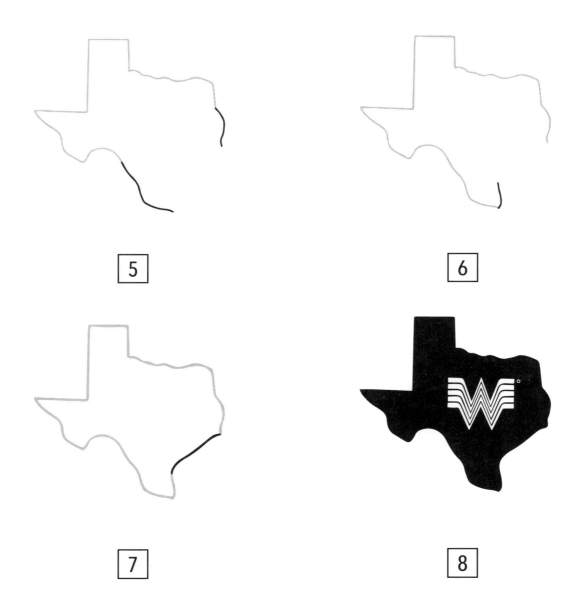

5

6

7

8

59

MONSTER TRUCK

The first monster truck was created in 1974 by Bob Chandler. It was called "Bigfoot."

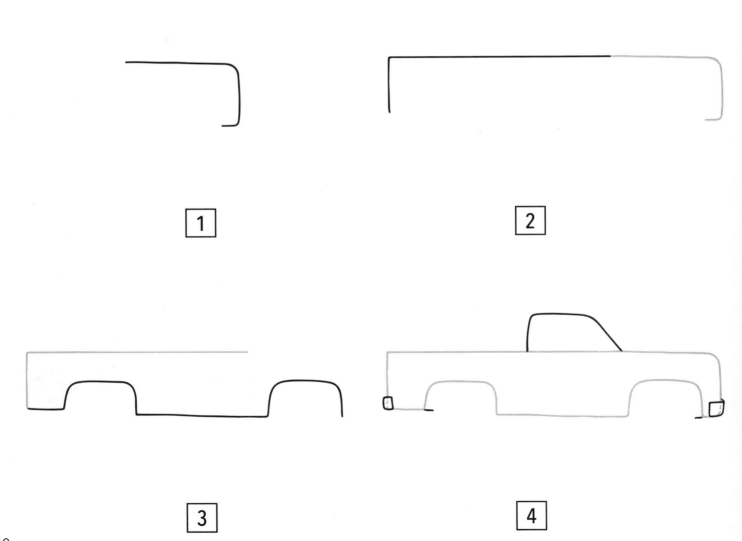

1

2

3

4

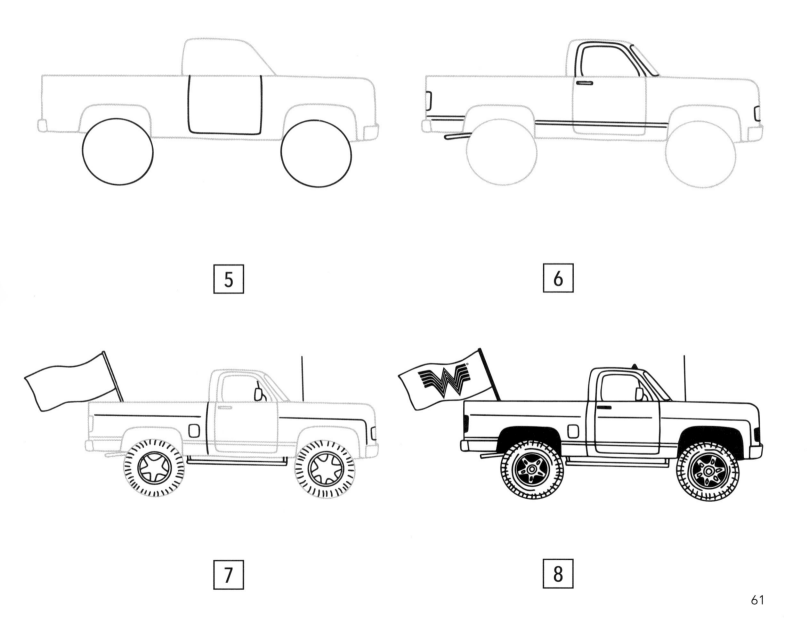

5

6

7

8

T-REX

The name Tyrannosaurus Rex comes from Greek and Latin words meaning "tyrant lizard king."

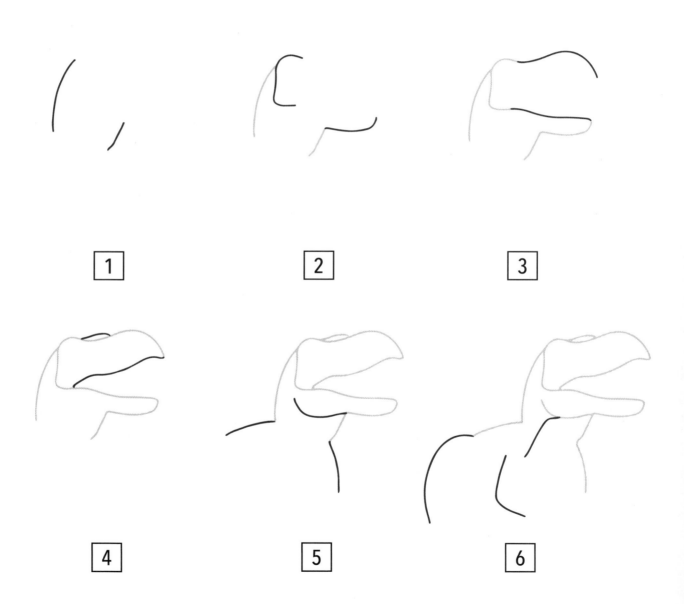

1

2

3

4

5

6

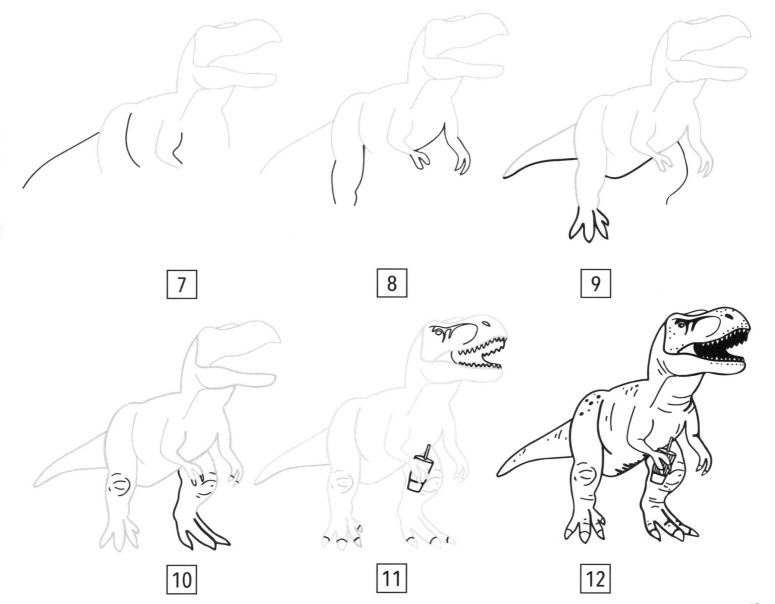

7

8

9

10

11

12

WHATAGUY

Whataburger's superhero mascot, Whataguy, first appeared on kids' meal bags and a games site in the summer of 1999. His mission is to protect freshness, flavor, and the Whataburger Way!

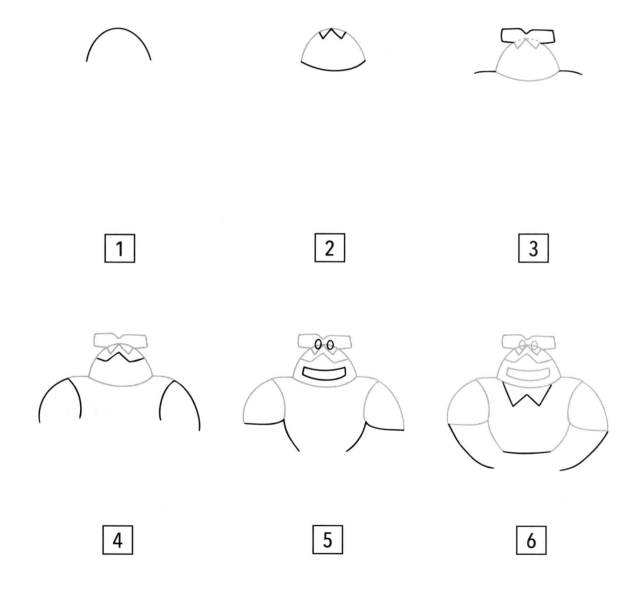

1

2

3

4

5

6

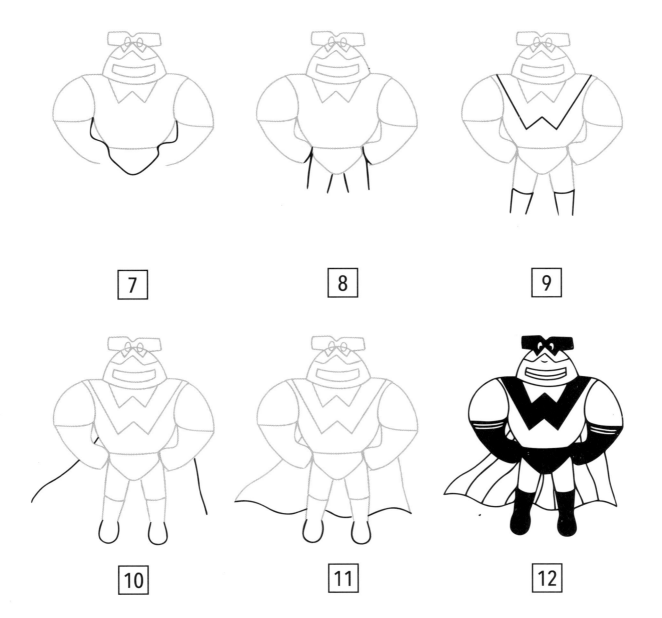

7

8

9

10

11

12

COWBOY HAT

Always store a cowboy hat upside down so it doesn't flatten or crease the brim!

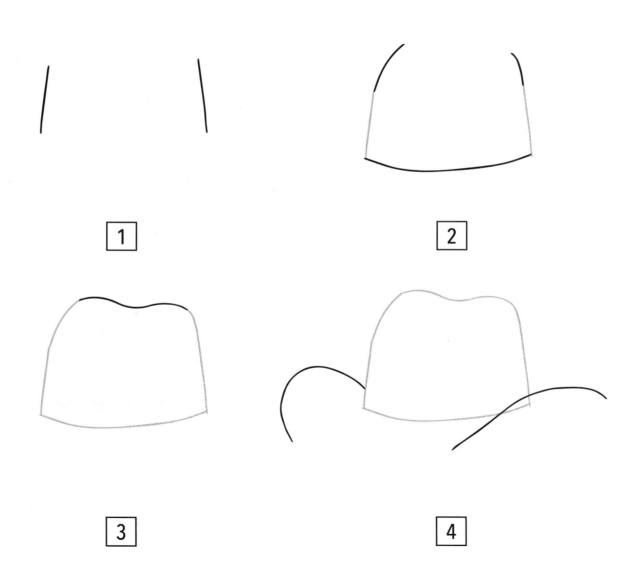

1

2

3

4

5

6

7

8

COWBOY BOOTS

The sturdy ends of the toes are designed to protect cowboys' feet from horse hooves.

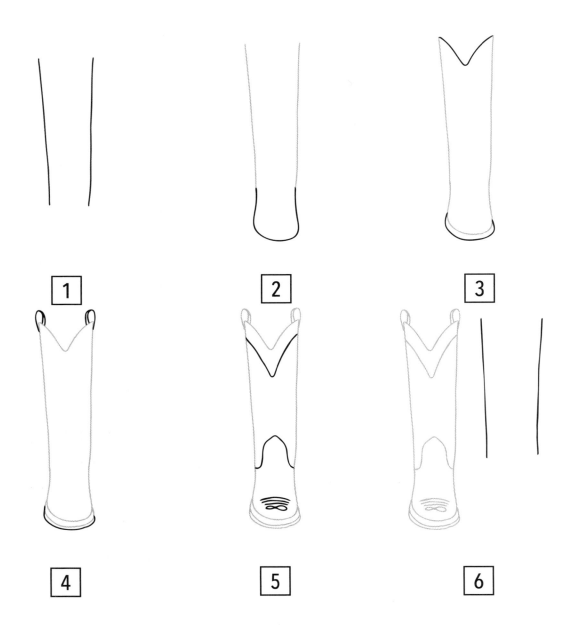

1

2

3

4

5

6

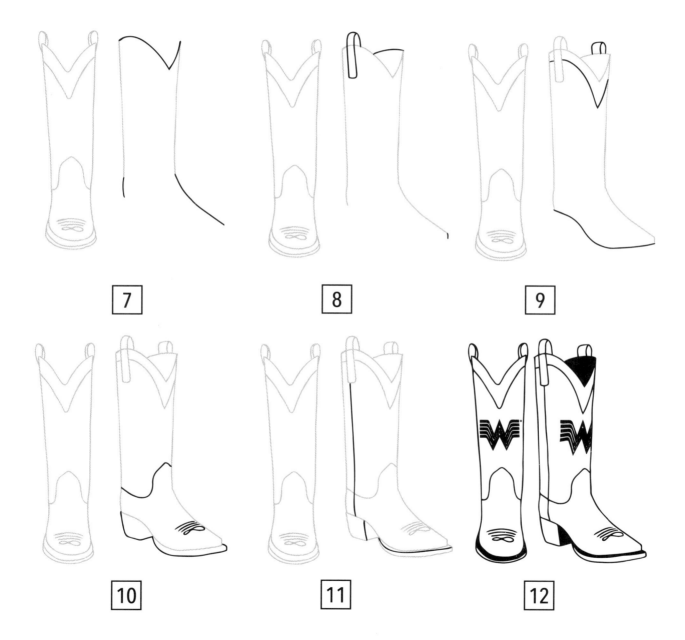

7

8

9

10

11

12

FOOTBALL

American pro football was invented in 1892, which means the sport is just a little over 100 years old.

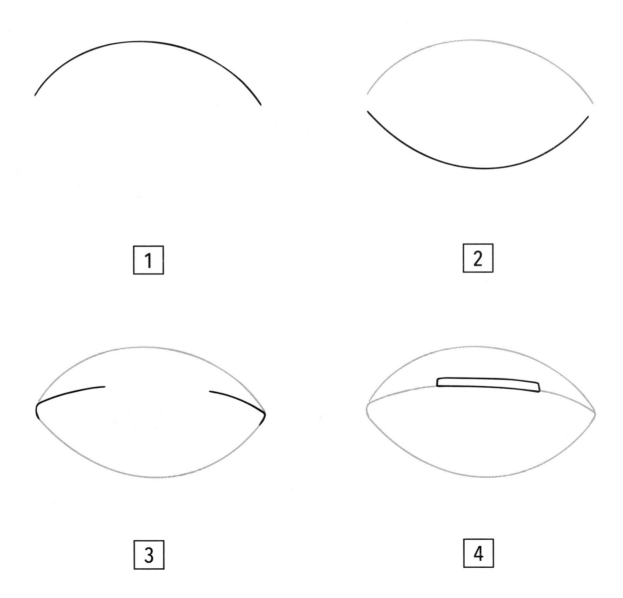

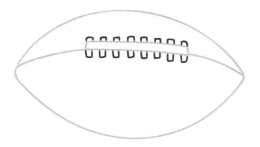

5

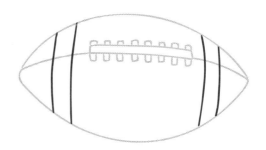

6

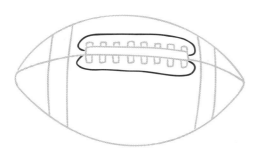

7

8

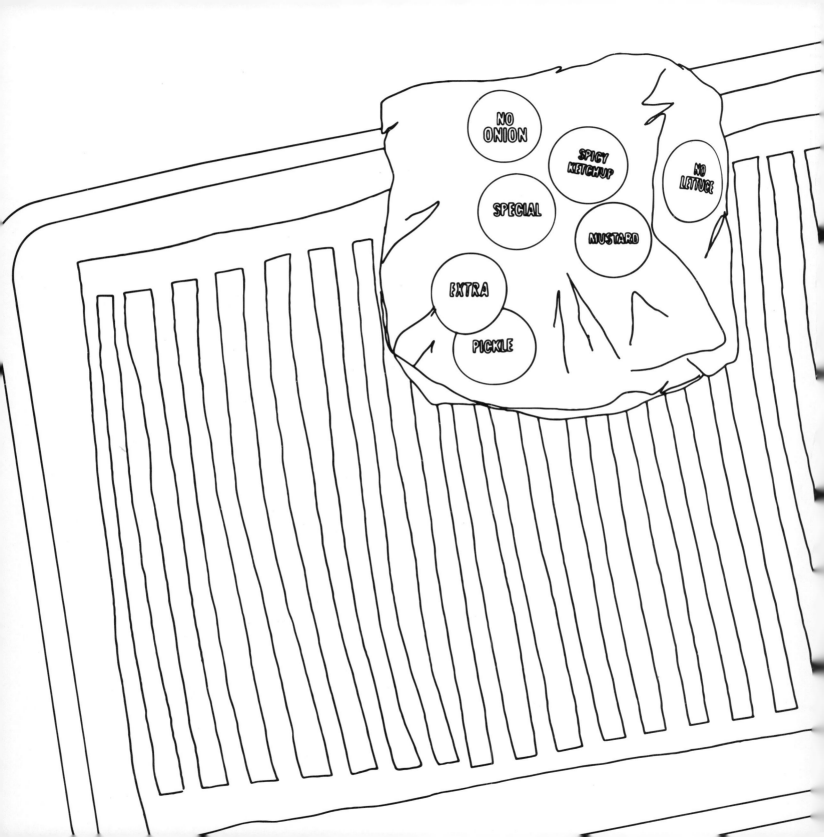

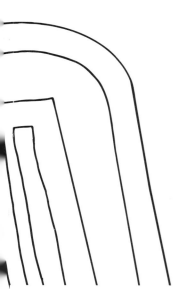

CREATE YOUR OWN

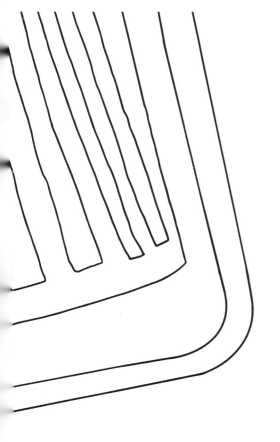

CREATE YOUR OWN BURGER

Use this page to create a burger how you would want it!

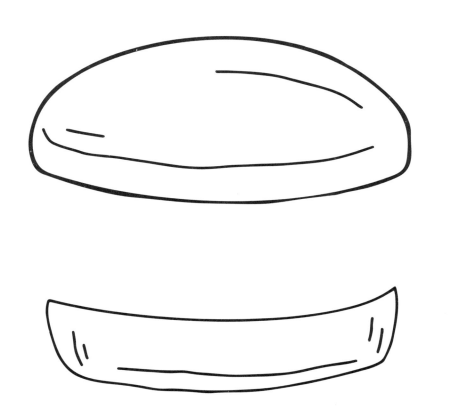

CREATE YOUR OWN SAUCE

Use this page to draw your favorite sauce or create your own secret sauce!

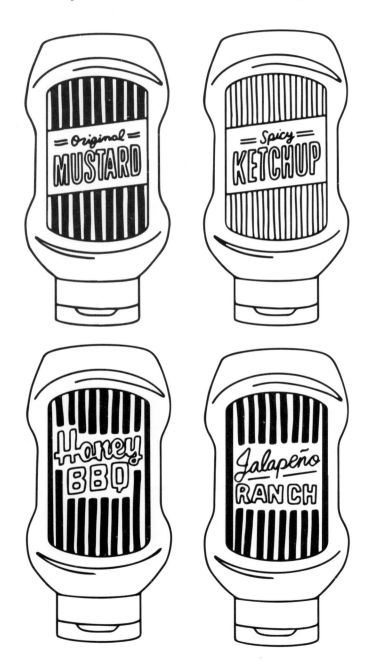

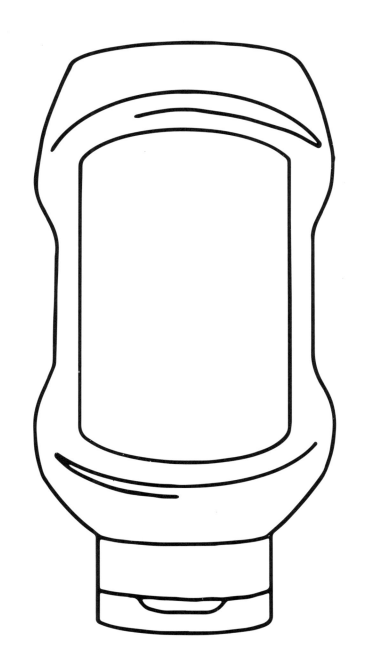

CREATE YOUR OWN FOOD ORDER

Use this page to draw your favorite Whataburger order!

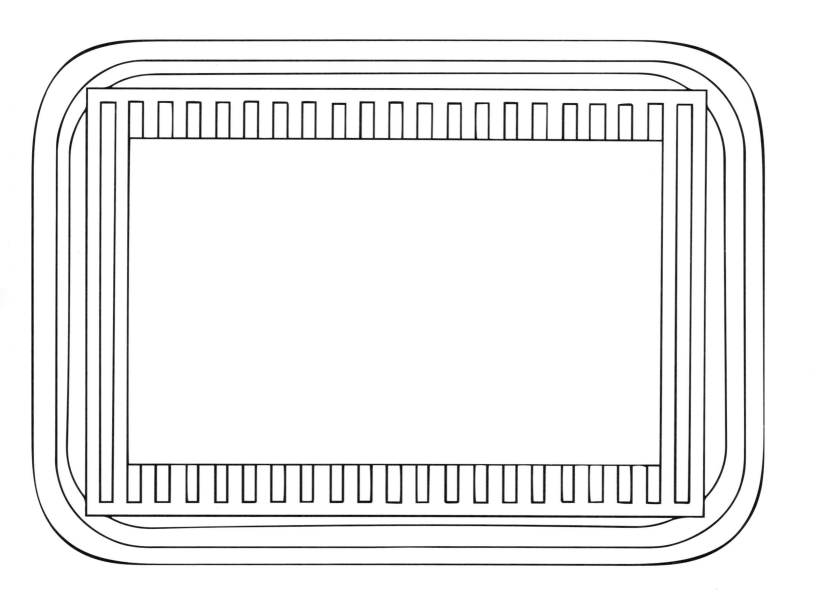

About Alli K

NAME: Alli Koch

HOME: Dallas, Texas

BIRTHDAY: March 20, 1991

FAVORITE COLOR: Black

WHATABURGER FAVORITE: Spicy ketchup and fries!

JOB: I am a full-time artist! I sell my art online, paint murals on the side of buildings, and teach others how to draw or be creative.

FAVORITE THING: A warm blanket

PETS: I have one cat named Emmie

CAR: Two-door Jeep

FAMILY: Married to my high school sweetheart

FAVORITE THING TO DO: Play board games!